Orbs Speak

HOW BEINGS
FROM ANOTHER DIMENSION
ARE HELPING TRANSFORM
HUMAN CONSCIOUSNESS

First published in 2008
by William Bloom – Holistic Partnerships
PO Box 2809 Glastonbury
Somerset BA6 8XQ UK
www.williambloom.com

Category: New Age/Mythology

ISBN 978-0-9559379-0-3

Cover design and book styling: Bernard Chandler
www.graffik.co.uk

Contents

Author's Note

In 1987 I began to experience a voice in my head which went on to communicate the material in this book. I have written many books, both fiction and non-fiction, and have never had a similar experience. The process was enjoyable and educational. In 2008, in preparation for a conference on Orbs, I received a further communication that it was Orbs who had telepathically transmitted the book to me.

I know very well that there is a body of scientific evidence which suggests that the many photographs of Orbs are, in fact, the result of dust and water particles. There are other scientific explanations too.

From my perspective, it does not matter whether the Orbs depicted in the photographs are 'real' or not. This would start too long a conversation on what is real anyway. As it is, Orbs provide a loving gateway for many people into a mythic and multidimensional world. This other world has a validity and integrity of its own. In the realms of consciousness all things are possible.

Some of the material presented here was published in another version as *The Christ Sparks* by the Findhorn Press in 1995. This material has been substantially clarified and there are also additions, in particular the final communication about our current environmental challenges.

I wish you all love.

William Bloom
Glastonbury June 2008

ORBS SPEAK

1

The Avatar of Synthesis and The Orbs

We are many units of consciousness, not simply one. We work as if we were a cloud or a flock.

Our method of communicating is to touch people's energy fields. We do this so that you begin to experience yourselves in a new way. Your new experience, which is triggered by us, is to sense that you are like us — not just individuals but a collective, a flock.

We are a swarm. We work together and have total rapport.

We work as one form. As we touch your individual psyches you begin consciously to experience yourselves as intimately connected with all other life-forms on this planet and throughout the Cosmos.

Our purpose in being here upon this planet is to support group consciousness.

Group consciousness is a subject which is crucial yet not properly understood. We want to share about how group consciousness is now available to humanity at this time.

We also want to communicate about another great consciousness who began incarnating into this planet in the 1960s but who prepared for it long before. This consciousness is sometimes known as the Avatar of Synthesis.

This being is a consciousness belonging to realms

beyond this galaxy and beyond these limited dimensions of time and space. We also come from there. We do not want to stimulate thoughts about unidentified flying objects or extra-terrestrial beings. We are talking here about energy states and multidimensional modes of consciousness that are only now becoming a part of Earth's and humanity's experience.

People call into their lives events and relationships to help them grow and develop. In the same way, Earth, nature and humanity have sounded out a call for support. The need for help is clear. Earth is increasing its human population. New technological and industrial systems are dominating.

There is a response to that call for support and it comes from another part of the Cosmos.

This response creates an energy event and a new relationship with consciousness.

The Avatar of Synthesis is just such a cosmic being responding to humanity's call. Its first points of contact started in the 1960s, in particular through certain spiritual communities such as Findhorn in Scotland and Auroville in India.

We also responded to the call. At the same time that the Avatar of Synthesis incarnated, we incarnated alongside it. We are separate from the Avatar of Synthesis. We have a particular history and experience, which enable us to work co-operatively with the Avatar of Synthesis and to serve humanity.

We are units of consciousness similar to human souls, except that the human soul is more rounded and individualistic than we are. We do not have the depth of individual history that human souls have.

We have a consciousness and group mind which is able

to understand the whole pattern of circumstances and impulses in any situation or event.

We experience and understand all the connections and relationships very easily. That is our nature.

We have evolved as a swarm and not as individuals.

We are by our very nature *electric,* electric sparks of consciousness. We exist as tingles of awareness, dancing. We have our own experience and own history, but our work now is to help that stream of evolution which is congested in time, space and individuality — you. We do this work for our evolution too.

Human consciousness, by its very nature, has to proceed through time and space as if in a tunnel. We do not experience that tunnel. We experience ourselves as waves in eternity. Like angelic lives we simultaneously know the beginning and the end. We experience this in a transcendent dimension which is separate from the tunnel that is your form of passing through time and space.

As we incarnate into Earth we have a clear sense of the patterns of co-operation which can exist between all human beings. We understand and perceive here and now that all consciousness on this planet is intimately interlinked.

Now this is an idea — that all life and consciousness are interlinked — which is mainly an intellectual idea for humanity. It is mainly an ideology. It needs also to be an experience and a state of being.

Our experience of the interdependence of life upon this planet is not intellectual or romantic. It is an active sensation and knowing, and we want all human beings to participate in this reality.

Our evolution is similar to the group soul of a nest of ants, swarm of bees or flock of birds. Our particular mode of evolution has meant that we retain our unity within a group soul yet have become self-conscious in the same way that humans are self-conscious. Thus we achieve self-consciousness at the same time as being part of a group. We achieve self-awareness while still remaining aware of our intimate connections as manifestations of the same group soul.

2

Why is there Human Separation?

In this section we want to discuss the history of human consciousness as seen from the soul's perspective.

It is of course true that all souls emerged out of the one cosmic soul.

In dimensions of consciousness that are more dynamic and fluid than everyday human awareness, all consciousness experiences unity. But this sense of unity is not the nature of your everyday knowing.

In your everyday knowing, you do not experience yourselves as being part of one interconnected network throbbing with the life of the one cosmic soul.

Nor do you mainly experience yourselves as cells organically connected in one wonderful cosmic creature.

The full experience of interconnectedness is one that usually only comes in heightened moments of awareness, peaks of connection. And then this heightened awareness of connection is lost the moment that you return to your everyday stimulation.

Even then, if you remember your connection or find it significant, your main thoughts and feelings are towards your connection with nature or with God. In the very fabric of your psyches you rarely feel and think that you are one with all other human beings. The main effect of your experience of Oneness is to feel closer to the source of spirit.

Experiences of connection lead you forward on your idea of the spiritual path. You instinctively attempt to move faster down the tunnel of time and space towards what you may call God.

But in this writing we want to describe the beginning of a new process in which spiritual connection is more than a path to the divine. It includes connection and spiritual solidarity with all life upon the planet, including all human life. Not just as an idea, but as a felt knowing.

Most of you have this connected experience with nature. Throughout aeons, your species has experienced its fellowship with nature.

Even though she can be savage and dangerous, most of you nevertheless feel connection and beauty with her. You are touched by your cellular resonance with all natural life upon the planet. Sometimes you may feel the same way about your close relations and families. Depending upon your history and personality, you may have a stronger sense of harmony and unity with minerals — or landscape — or plants — or animals.

But there is a gap.

On one side you feel unity with spirit.

On the other side you feel unity with nature.

In between there is humanity with whom most people do not experience unity.

What we are describing here is a new experience — a genuine sense of unity with all human life. The possibility of ecstatic wholeness with all humanity.

We want to describe it not as an idea or a romance, but as an experience which may throb through every cell of your psyche and body.

Humanity is one, and each of you are one with it.

○

We wish to focus now on exactly why it is that individual humans — no matter how powerful and pure their devotion, no matter how powerful and pure their aspiration towards a sense of unity — nevertheless have difficulty experiencing this unity with their fellow beings.

Let us be clear that the major pattern which has to be transcended here is one of fear. This fear has ancient historical sources.

It is not the experience of most human beings that your fellow creatures are to be trusted. It is not the ongoing minute-by-minute experience of most human beings that you can surrender yourselves in trust to all your fellows.

What is the source of this separation?

Why do you not feel the same way about each other as you feel about nature and spirit?

Let us be clear that the molecules and atoms of your body also belong to, have come from, and will return to the bodies of minerals, plants, animals and other humans. Imprinted in the molecular patterns of your body are memories and vibrations that belong to the mineral, plant, animal and human realms. The consciousness and vibrations of the different kingdoms are locked into the human body.

You can, if you want, tap into the memory and states of those other kingdoms. You can, if you want, take your awareness through the cells of your own body into the consciousness of the mineral kingdom. Through that rapport you can find knowledge which was previously inaccessible to you.

This sense of unity with the mineral kingdom, through attunement to its vibration in your own body, is just the seed of an intimate connection which you can consciously develop into something deeper. Humanity has hardly developed the potential of these connections.

Your human molecular make-up, however, does not hold such a harmonious resonance with your fellow humans. You are more able to vibrate harmoniously with animals, plants and minerals than with people. Why is this so?

There is a history here that is to do with the earliest evolution of humanity when apes became human, when the human psyche emerged. This is esoteric history.

O

The human psyche was born through a marriage. This marriage was between highly developed apes and spiritual waves or jewels that come from another dimension of the Cosmos.

As the physiology and energy field of the apes met these Cosmic entities a new fire arose in their mind-brains — human consciousness. In the same way that fire emerges when wood is rubbed fast, so human consciousness arose from the heated friction of the energy fields of the ape meeting the energy fields of the incoming spiritual jewels.

These apes who were brought into human consciousness were attracted to congregate at specific areas upon the surface of the planet where natural vortices of energy exist. These vortices made it possible to bring the apes' energy fields and brains up to a vibrational peak of such intensity that they could connect with and receive the incoming spiritual jewels. The apes and the cosmic jewels merged.

These jewels, like angelic life-forms, hold within themselves the whole pattern, or plan, of both their history and their unfoldment. They have cosmic consciousness. But when they incarnated into human apes, they become caught in time-space-form and lost their cosmic awareness.

These jewels are human souls.

○

When these souls first began to incarnate, they were responding to the needs of Earth. Just as we Orbs do now.

In those times, millions of years ago, the development of Earth was moving in a rhythm that could be described as too slow. A potential for change was being held back. Because of Earth's relationship with other planets, solar and star systems, this 'slowness' had implications through its constellation and beyond.

Left alone, it is possible that the apes might have slowly evolved into a new form of consciousness. However, at that time Earth held a significant role in the evolution of the systems in which she is a part. Earth was then, and is still now, a pivot for cosmic changes concerning matter and consciousness. In the future, as in the distant past, Earth will not hold such an important role; but she does now.

The relative slowness of the evolution of the apes' consciousness was problematic. It created a tension. This tension could be described as similar to the travail of a woman going through the pains of childbirth. It was a painful labour that was taking too long.

One can talk about a point in Earth's history when the mineral, plant and animal realms were struggling with the effort of pushing forward the evolution of the apes.

The psyche of the planet sounded out this note of labour. There is Divine Justice and the response came in the form of the jewels of spirit — the souls — who were attracted to incarnate into these apes on Earth.

This was a dramatic intervention. Over several centuries, these souls were brought into Earth's aura and incarnated into the aura of these highly evolved animals, the sophisticated apes.

Conscious self-awareness — the major attribute of a human being — came about through the incarnation of the soul into the ape. Human consciousness, the human psyche, is the result of this marriage between ape and spirit.

○

The issue arises as to why these ape-people were evolving so slowly in the first place and why Earth was experiencing such travail. It is difficult for human minds to consider the possibility of mistakes in cosmic evolution. But in understanding this history you will come closer to understanding why human evolution includes so much misery and suffering along with so much creativity, love and genius.

The reason for the slowness of the apes' evolution and of Earth's painful labour lies in ancient cosmic history when various great consciousnesses — Gods — experimented with the solar system before this one that you currently inhabit. This experimentation was temporarily unsuccessful and left behind energy-matter-consciousness which had been 'stretched' too fast and 'collapsed'.

This is not to say that Ultimate Reality plays games, only that there is sufficient freedom within the system for temporary 'mistakes' or congestions. And then, through love and responsibility, they are healed.

Crucially, from your perspective, this 'failed' material is the 'stuff' that makes up the physical, pranic, emotional and mental material of planet Earth. This stuff — the collapsed material from a 'failed' previous system —makes up your bodies, emotions, thoughts and energy fields.

Souls then incarnated into this material in order to re-vibrate it. Your souls were attracted into Earth and incarnated into ape-people in order to bring everything back into harmony. They were magnetically drawn into a situation that needed them.

O

As far as we are aware, this particular situation is unique to planet Earth and not present in any other parts of the Cosmos.

This is also why Earth and humanity are developing a unique form of consciousness. Earth is the place where the mistake of a previous system is being rectified. This is why human beings experience both suffering and joy to such extremes.

This is why what you call 'aliens' do indeed have an interest in Earth. They are interested in this highly unusual form of consciousness found in human beings and usually only available to much more evolved beings.

This uniquely human experience of both joy and suffering has resulted in an unusual level of *compassion.*

Compassion is an attitude and a vibration which usually exists only at very high levels of consciousness. Humanity, given its current level in cosmic evolution, is unusual in its demonstration of compassion. In the rest of the cosmos, what you on Earth know as compassion is a state of being that belongs only to those more evolved consciousnesses who have the status of Gods and Goddesses.

Before we came to Earth we, the Orbs, were unaware of compassion. We have learnt about it since we landed and it has been a very important part of our own growth. We now consider ourselves honoured and sanctified to have been able to integrate compassion into our own consciousness and experience.

O

The mineral, animal and plant kingdoms, unique and extraordinary, exist in harmony with each other on Earth. There is a natural chain and cycle between them, a natural form of co-operation, a natural form of rhythmic dancing existence, which reflects the basic harmonies of the Cosmos as a whole.

These harmonies on Earth were, however, partly shattered when the first souls incarnated and the ape-people were initiated into self-aware human consciousness. The vibration carried by the incarnating souls excited the ape-people's brain cells and nervous systems in a way never previously experienced. The electricity of the souls, encountering the electricity of the ape-people, created a new electricity. This new electricity, this new fire, was the seed of self-awareness and self-knowledge. Its vibration was not soothing and easy, but caused a form of electric irritation in the brain and nervous system.

The immediate result was not harmonious.

The beginning of self-awareness was disturbing and irritating for the new humans. They became self-aware of themselves and of nature, became confused, disorientated and frightened. They temporarily lost the harmonies derived simply from the joy of being alive.

Previously there had been a harmonious, unconscious acceptance of interdependence and the cycles of birth-life-death-rebirth. This new self-awareness brought humans an irritating and threatening awareness of *self-otherness*. This brought difficulties.

This new awareness and internal friction produced dissonance and fear.

The primal images of early humans, frightened in the forests and jungles, hiding in the trees, seeking safety in caves and in heights, are accurate and poignant.

It was indeed at this time that external beings introduced the gift of making fire in order that the light and heat should bring your species some comfort and control in an environment which they now found hostile.

As apes you did not find the environment hostile because you were inextricably part of the rhythms and cycles of nature. Now self-aware of your own limitations and mortality, you were painfully conscious of your own vulnerability.

This vulnerability was experienced in relation to all the kingdoms upon the planet. The earth itself was unsafe in all sorts of ways — earth tremors, openings in the ground, volcanoes and so on. The plants themselves were also threatening because many of them were poisonous.

Previously there had been a natural rhythmic dance between ape-people and plants, and they knew instinctively which plants to eat. Now there were the beginnings of an inability to judge what was appropriate to eat and poisonings happened. With the animal realm, there were many obvious physical threats.

Nevertheless at a molecular level inside the new humans, there still existed the memories of the harmonic relationship with the other kingdoms. In the molecular make-up of the human bodies was the locked-in memory of the divine dance with these other kingdoms — a dance that was beautiful and comforting in its ecological wholeness and appropriateness.

There was not, however, any memory of a similar harmonious relationship with their fellow human beings.

This is a crucial piece of historical information for understanding why human beings do not have the same instinctive experience of oneness with other human beings.

The reader can see, therefore, that from the very beginning of human consciousness, locked into the collective human experience, there was no molecular memory of harmony with fellow human beings — because this harmony had not previously existed. There was only memory of harmony with the mineral, plant and animal realms.

○

These early human beings were vulnerable.

There was competition to survive in any given ecological space. Any given area could only sustain a certain population of hunter-gatherers.

Also, as in other parts of the animal realms, there was competition concerning mating.

There was, too, the prolonged vulnerability of the human infant.

We have, therefore, a picture here of early human beings existing in a state of anxiety concerning each other. It is in the very essence of human history that there are difficulties in co-operating and that anxiety is experienced in human relations.

Whereas there is a subconscious molecular memory of co-operation and symbiosis with the mineral, plant and animal realms — there is no similar memory of co-operation with fellow humans.

However, in our opinion, the tragedy of this history is more than balanced by the human development of compassion and the capacity to love.

O

Now, we do not wish to say more at this moment about humanity's history. We want to jump forward into the very moments of the present.

Just as millions of years ago, the first souls incarnated to relieve the travail of evolution on Earth — so right now, Earth and humanity are experiencing a similar event.

We have mentioned already that the Avatar of Synthesis and we ourselves are forms of Cosmic consciousness who have responded to the call of Earth and her realms.

Our way of being and doing, and the nature of the Avatar of Synthesis, can help to heal the sense of separation which exists between human beings. We are sparks of spirit — belonging to cosmic consciousness — and we carry the redemptive energy field of group awareness and unconditional love.

Earlier we described the nature of our consciousness and how we are individuals within the awareness of a group soul, a swarm, a shoal. We bring into the human psyche — as we come close to you — a healing and a new sense of adventure, co-operation and loving synthesis with all human beings upon Earth.

We want to underline that this demands no loss of individuality nor of the many eccentric forms of human personality that currently exist among you. You retain your individuality. At the same time you will enjoy being part of your community, your swarm.

We are talking about a new form of calm, a new form of ease.

In your bodies there is that molecular memory of

harmony and co-operation with mineral, animal and plant realms.

Now we bring a vibration and awareness that sings into the molecules of human beings the experience of loving co-operation with fellow humans.

3

Couples as Communities

In this section we want to move into discussing certain aspects which we hope will be of immediate practical help.

We want to look at the problems faced in relationships, couples and marriages. The guidelines for relationships have been changing over the last century.

The major guideline that is now being applied to serious relationships is that they need to serve the psychological and spiritual growth of the people involved.

When a close relationship is no longer serving personal and spiritual development, it is probably time to end it.

This is appropriate. It is also, in some ways, new.

We want to help clarify the difference between relationships now and in the past.

Before that, however, we want you to notice the responsibility that is incurred when a couple choose to have children. The relationship of parent is enduring. We look forward to a time in human society when there will be contracts for parenting, alongside the usual pledges for marriage. We want no situation where a child is parented by a single being. We look forward to when there is true community of responsibility for children. Our essential instinct is for collective awareness. We are individual beings within a swarm.

O

Why are relationships so difficult?

In the past, couples came together for procreation and to satisfy sexual needs. This was sanctified and marked by social and religious rituals. This ensured the stability of the society in which the relationship took place and also the continuity of parenting.

In a sense, society and religion owned marriage. Marriage was a social commitment and a religious institution. This idea is far from marriage being simply a playful union of sexual connection between two human beings following their natural instincts.

If you combine that social and religious control with the anxiety human beings already hold for each other, you have a recipe for further tension. It is all contrary to a naturally harmonious flow of affection and playful relationship. It is natural as creatures that you would want to liberate yourselves from those constraints.

It is natural that men and women should want relationships that are more open and loving. Also, as the planetary psyche moves out of the cycle of Pisces into the cycle of Aquarius, new forms of relationship are emerging.

More than that, the incarnation forty years ago of the Avatar of Synthesis and of we Orbs also creates new dynamics, which are to a large degree responsible for the chaos of modern relationships.

The challenges of relationship cannot be underestimated.

Your expectations of relationship are being shattered.

You have been brought up with certain images of how you should behave in relationships and certain images of the commitment you should give. You now find yourselves in maturity acting in ways that are in conflict with these inner images of yourselves.

Working with you, we want to create new forms of relationship filled with self-respect, integrity, loyalty and love.

○

[At this stage in the dictation the Orbs changed subject and began to describe themselves in more detail. They then returned to the subject of couples and relationships.]

We have already spoken about the fact that the nature of our form of consciousness is as a swarm. That although we are individual units of consciousness we inter-relate in a way that is totally group self-aware, that is naturally and continuously, second by second, aware of each other's experience.

We would like you to imagine us for the moment as a cellular network. Imagine each cell within this network as having a completely separate and unique consciousness, a completely separate and unique life history, life present and life future. Yet we are all bound together in our acknowledgement and knowing of our unity within the one creative breath that brought us all into being. And we are all bound together within the knowledge that we move in time in the broad sweep of space to a state of pure Spirit.

Yet as we pass through time and space through our own forms of self-reflective awareness, we move through moods and states and feelings that are not of pure Spirit, but that resonate with our materialistic base.

Imagine that one cell or psyche amongst us is brought into resonance with its own materialism. Part of the Orb is resonant with materialism — or egoism; part of the Orb is resonant with Spirit. In that moment, the Orb feels confusion and friction which takes it into a spin of dissonance. That dissonance echoes out, vibrates out, through the cellular network of which it is a part, and we are all aware of it. At the same time that Orb is aware of all of us.

We as a swarm absorb its confusion, while at the same time that Orb absorbs from us our clarity concerning its Spirit. You can see, therefore, that there is virtually no time-lag between its experience of confusion and its experience of our comforting it. They happen simultaneously. We hope that you begin to catch here an understanding of a network of supportive natural love and of open awareness held resonant with higher consciousness.

Imagine that one of the Orbs, through its own particular dance and process, becomes blissfully ecstatic in any particular moment. This is immediately connected through the whole of the network and we are all aware of that state with the Orb who is experiencing it. The Orb, in its sanctified and graceful state, blesses all of us simultaneously in the precise moment that it is experiencing its grace. We would like you to recognise the point we made before, that none of this in any way affects or denigrates the individuality of the unique Orb having its own experience. It does however, mean that we are all in that moment when the events are happening, experiencing its experience. The interlinking is intimate and immediate.

Within the occult teaching available to humanity there is a clear notion of the interrelationship and telepathic rapport of all life. But it is not immediate, nor is it cellular in the way that the Orbs exist. The mystic experience, ecstasy, has a form for you. It is like a chalice that overflows with the mystical experience and flows out to other people, and is felt and absorbed by them. This is different from the way in which the Orbs immediately experience, in full, each individual Orb's experience.

We would like you to understand that the changes happening in humanity at the moment are bringing you into the same experience of life that we Orbs enjoy.

○

Now look at where a unified field of consciousness may manifest at its most intimate. It is within a man and a woman, or same genders, coming together to couple.

If they are both in any way interested in spiritual growth, they immediately enter the new vibrations and consciousness which we are bringing into incarnation.

Our state affects them.

As a couple they are no longer distinct and separate units interacting with each other. We the Orbs have incarnated and vibrated into their psyches an instantaneous and mutual empathy of experience.

In the intimacy of coupling, one person's natural spiritual growth — blissful ecstatic experience — is immediately communicated through to the psyche of the partner.

At the same time, when one individual in a couple experiences a downward spin or some form of anxiety or depression, this too is instantaneously communicated and experienced by the other.

We would like you to appreciate, that in this form of empathic experience, we are not talking about the communication of vibrations or the occult communication of energies that can depress. We are talking about empathic harmony, sympathetic resonance. If it happens within one person, it also happens *within* the other – and vice versa.

We would like to be clearer here: If a woman or a man comes into a room and is suffering severe depression and is radiating depressive vibrations, this may vibrationally affect everyone else in the room and depress them.

But when we talk about the instantaneous communication of depression from one member of a couple to the other, we do not mean a vibrational communication. We are talking about a shared awareness, a shared experience. It is as if you are inside each other.

This is similar to the relationship and experience between parents and their children. They can feel within themselves – through cellular empathy – the children's experience. When this happens also within couples, the possibility for mutual support and love is profound. This support may happen completely unconsciously.

One partner may, for example, feel a sense of depression and compensate with an instinctive action of self-healing. This, in turn, is experienced by the partner who was originally in the depressed mood.

From our perspective we find this graceful, stimulating and interesting. We are talking here about a form of empathic relationship not previously experienced by human beings for each other. It is similar to the way in which the Angelic realms communicate and experience each other.

All this is now accelerated for human beings because that is how we the Orbs experience life. Now we incarnate in you and you share our resonance as well as, subconsciously, our experience. We are like a benevolent virus.

O

In your mystical traditions, there was always an ideal that couples could form a spiritual community — a spiritual community of two. But that possibility is now far more intense and powerful.

At the same time this whole syndrome of mutual empathy provides increasingly difficult problems for the human personality.

We want to be very practical here and ask you to imagine a couple who have come together for one reason or another. They then come under the influence of the Avatar of Synthesis and of we Orbs. This could happen through visiting a spiritual community, taking part in some kind of workshop, being influenced by a book, or touching us privately in meditation. We Orbs are currently touching many hundreds of thousands of people, soon millions.

But look at this couple and the patterns they are carrying. Suddenly, they are brought into an intimate form of empathy and shared experience which they had not sought or expected.

Beforehand they had no idea how intense and intimate relationship can be. We Orbs amplify the experience.

This couple suddenly enters a new vibrational field and they are now drawn into this intimate new form of coupling. Their psyches are now experiencing each other as a swarm or as a single entity.

It is at this point that deeper layers of their psychologies surface and perhaps demonstrate the inappropriateness of their coupling. By the old laws — by the old reasons, rationalisations and justifications — it may seem absolutely perfect that they should be together. However, as we the Orbs bring group consciousness into their psyches, and draw them into these new forms of consciousness and empathy, it may become intensely obvious that their relationship lacks harmony. Their rhythms become dissonant. There is mutual alienation and they ask why this should be so.

You may demand a bit of logical clarity here. Why, when we the Orbs enter in the consciousness of a couple, does this not create greater mutual support and affection?

That may indeed happen, but we are not able to heal the deep-seated patterns of pain which exist in many human beings. We can bring a couple into empathic rapport with one another. Then, if they want, no matter how badly they may be getting on, they can call in healing energies and unconditional love.

But for many couples this is asking too much. They each have their own deep-seated rhythms and patterns of growth and change, and the two people cannot move hand in hand. It is as if one of them is running and one of them is skipping. Or in another couple, it is as if one of them may be happy doing a stomach crawl along the grass while carefully examining everything in the way, while the other one wishes to travel beneath a hang-glider.

With that kind of disparity, the empathic conflict is best ended with separation. They might previously have been totally compatible in terms of culture, intellect and social well-being, but our effect upon them may be to accelerate them into changes that demonstrate the inap-propriateness of the relationship.

Equally, when couples are brought into deeper rapport with each other through us, they can experience accelerated spiritual growth and psychological insight. This is because, in the new empathy, they may find a new form of bonding and safe affection. This gives them the most profound type of psychological security which allows them to accept lessons and insights which were hitherto deeply repressed. In the context of the new empathic support, they can work with psychological material that was previously too threatening.

O

Once our resonance touches the psyches of a couple,

they can begin to work and grow together in a far more intense form of empathetic rapport. They begin to function psychically as two cells within the same organism. They act as two clear identities, yet within one gestalt.

We should state here that the awareness which we bring will sooner or later be incarnate across the planet in all humanity. This will bring problems just as much as it brings blessings. Humanity as a whole and individually still has to work out its own karma.

We shall pursue the implications of all this for larger groups later on. We want to discuss couples first because we perceive an urgency for clarity about the problems in contemporary relationships. A question often put forward is: 'What are the rules for relationship?'

The primary responsibility of each individual — whether in a relationship or not — is to spiritually evolve. That does not stop when someone comes into a relationship. The purpose of relationship is to support spiritual evolution.

You need also to be responsible for your environment and recognise that within a relationship your immediate environment is your partner. *The immediate ecological responsibility you have is for your partner.* Within a couple it is best to be aware of the vibrations you radiate that affect your partner.

This requires a sensitive and caring attitude. In the same way that you are beginning to care for the Earth, you care for your partner.

If two people come together understanding and respecting that each other's primary purpose is to evolve spiritually, then you have the foundation for a healthy, respectful and ecstatic relationship.

O

As we Orbs, we Sparks, resonate into the psyches of couples we bring a new dynamic. This creates an energy field that belongs to them as a couple.

In their relationship there are now three energy fields: his, hers, theirs.

This means that the atmosphere created by a couple is intensified and amplified.

A couple needs now to be conscious and reflective about what it is that they are radiating out into their environment. We are not talking about obvious vibrational effects, for example from arguing or love-making. We are talking about the general magnetic effect that a couple has, which comes from the overall quality of their relationship. This is more subtle, but also deeper and more influential.

We are asking couples to be self-reflective about the general nature of their resonance. Couples need to recognise that they spend an immense amount of time together, more than they do with anyone else, if only by their bodies sleeping together at night.

Two people living together create a gestalt which is more than the sum of their individual lives put together. They need to take responsibility for this.

We are suggesting, therefore, that couples might reflect upon the nature of the atmosphere they communicate to their environment. We are actually asking couples to stop, pause and communicate together about this on a daily basis. We are talking here about couples attuning together. What are you as a couple radiating?

In the same way that some of you are meditating on a daily basis, or are taking silence together in communities on a daily or weekly basis, we are now talking about couples also attuning together on a daily basis. They can attune to their relationship and take spiritual responsibility.

We hope that it is self-evidently creative and constructive for couples to work in this way. The benefits, in terms of a more responsible attitude both to themselves as individuals, to themselves as a couple, and to their environment, are obvious.

Moreover, this form of daily attunement and careful awareness given to what it is that they are radiating can help bring about a new psychological harmony, understanding and emotional goodwill. This can help melt emotional and other challenges which couples may experience.

O

The guidelines for couples are really quite simple. We shall repeat some of the statements we have just made and add nuances we think are relevant:

First, respect and support each other's individual spiritual growth.

Second, take responsibility for how you affect your partner. Your partner is your first environmental responsibility.

Third, be aware of what you radiate as a couple — and be aware of this by taking daily attunement and by reflecting together upon it.

Fourth, be aware that you are 'married' so as to work through and melt the patterns you bring with you. There is no point in being in the intense vortex of a coupling situation unless you take the opportunity to work consciously on your development.

We acknowledge, however, that the nature of this exercise — a couple daily attuning and talking together about what they, as individuals and together, radiate — can intensify the psychological challenges of relationship. It forces couples to address each other in an intimate way which can spiral into difficult atmospheres. As we Orbs become more aware and attuned to the human condition we realise that we ourselves may be naive in our expectations. We may lack a certain realism about human emotions.

○

We can imagine you asking us about what to do when relationships start to go wrong.

We can present no general rules for when and how relationships should either begin or end. We would state, however, that in terms of beginnings we would ask only that couples approach each other always within an atmosphere of intuitive knowing that their coupling is appropriate and with affection.

In terms of endings, we understand fully that there are painful problems here. We do suggest, however, that if couples would attune together on a daily basis and discuss what it is that they are radiating together — and as they do this to melt through the emotional and mental hooks that bind them painfully to each other — that they will then be able to move more gracefully into the future.

○

We play through you. Do you not see that it is all changed, all changing? We love you. We love everyone and everything. We are Orbs working with Christ/Buddha/ Cosmic Consciousness.

4

Groups, Communities and Politics

We have described the manner in which our incarnation affects couples. In the same way, we affect the empathic and energetic dynamics in groups of more than two people, especially if the purpose of that group has a spiritual aspect.

When people come together to work on a project, the project itself is less important than the energy and gestalt which the group creates

This may seem contradictory because when a group comes together, for example, to build a house or materialise any project, it seems that it is the actual house or project that matters. This is not the case. What matters is the energy and vibration with which it is all done.

The project may well be one that is of explicit service to the community, but we are concerned with the essence — the inner life or subjectivity — of the project.

It is a standard statement of esoteric teaching that all forms are but the manifestation of energetic ideas. All esoteric work is based on the understanding that the invisible world of ideas precipitates manifestation. The inner dimension is first and the manifestation second.

Just as the project was conceived out of thought and imagination, so the energies of thought and imagination continue as the project is materialised.

When a group comes together to create and build something, it is the atmosphere, the mood that they create as they work, which is crucial.

In many spiritual communities, any form of group work is preceded by moments of silent attunement. The purpose of these periods of silence is to bring the group members into harmony with each other and into harmony with the project.

Most groups, as soon as they begin to work, lose their sense of attunement to the inner dynamics. They focus on the material job in hand. But whatever is happening in the material world, emotions, feelings, thoughts and energies are still being radiated into the atmosphere. This invisible radiation is happening whether or not the workers are aware of it.

It has certainly been the ideal of many spiritual communities to work with an awareness of the spiritual harmony and radiate a blessing as they work.

With the incarnation of the Avatar of Synthesis the inner nature of group work has been intensified. The opportunity now exists for you to be aware of a new rapport and synergy.

It is now possible for groups to move with great speed through psychological and spiritual healing processes which might previously have taken many years. It is now possible for new groups to come together and, usually in silence, move immediately into a sense of healing connection, into the zone of healing and connection. This was not possible before.

It is possible now because of the incarnation of the Avatar of Synthesis and we Orbs. We bring to human beings an immediate empathic rapport. Strangers can join together and if they are prepared spiritually to open themselves to each other, they can pass quickly into a harmonic, support-ive and healing connection. There are many groups who are experiencing this.

When individuals come into group work, it is good if they prepare themselves in advance to be connected with the people with whom they are working. We are asking that people prepare for group work with the appro-priate psychological and energetic attitude.

We are asking people to open themselves up to real group experience. Open up. Take off your pyschic armour. Do not hold back. It is no longer necessary to be defended.

We are suggesting, with sensitivity to the pain and dif-ficulties you have experienced in the past, that it is possible for you to be completely open, in your own private and dis-crete manner, with the members of your group.

Imagine the harmony and encouragement that can exist in a group that comes together with this shared attitude. Imagine a group of women and men coming together to build a house, to fulfil a certain project. Before they come into the group, each one of them affirms that in the day to come, "I am open. I am open to synergy and co-operation with my fellow workers."

Now imagine that every worker on a project affirms these words or something similar before coming to work. Imagine that when they actually get together that they pause as a group and affirm their synergy and co-operation. We suggest that individuals hold that attitude within groups even if it is not shared by others. If just one person in a group adopts this approach, then he or she can have a great influence for good.

Now, imagine that the whole group comes together sharing that attitude. It can create grounded harmony in the workplace.

This harmony is supported by the rapport of Orbs. We bring a sense of fruition and calm. We bring a sense of the cellular solidarity of humans working together. This is in resonance with the universal harmonics of creation and manifestation.

We can therefore suggest that, as with couples, there are certain guidelines for individuals in group work:

First, before coming into group work, privately attune to the work and the group and affirm your synergy with them.

Second, be aware at work that you are with fellow souls, all on the path of spiritual growth and your real work is to support their development.

Third, be aware at work of the energy and attitudes that you radiate into your work environment and how they can affect your companions. Monitor and manage your vibrations.

Fourth, as a group take regular time together to sit in a relaxed and quiet way; and then share with each other as friends and colleagues. One thread of the conversation can be about the vibrations that the whole group is radiating into their environment.

O

Now that we have spent some time discussing couples and groups, we would like to pass on to the more complex subject of our effect upon communities. By communities we mean groups of anything from one hundred and fifty people upwards, through to larger political communities — from villages to nation-states — and finally the world community.

It is obvious when we are discussing communities of this size that the nature of the interaction between the individuals cannot be as intimate as that between individuals in couples and small groups. It is difficult for the attunements that can happen in small groups to be copied in large societies. Nevertheless they do happen in their own way.

In Europe, for example, national communities tend to pause to attune together. In a weekly rhythm, national communities take a breathing space on Sundays, particularly Sunday mornings. The whole country can be experienced as more quiet and calm. People who are aware of this calm can, in meditation, energetically work to create more connection and harmony through the national community. It is possible to tune into the needs of the community members – a village, street, town, nation, continent. In meditation you can visualise and sense a web of energy connecting all the people. You can radiate calm, nurture and healing into that web. You can build energetic community.

Just as couples or small groups radiate their own distinctive vibration, so too do larger communities and societies. It is difficult for the larger societies to pause and become self-aware of their atmosphere. There is however a form of communion and rapport that happens telepathically, into which you can radiate your own blessing and calm.

You can build up your awareness of your national web and care for it.

O

It is possible to work in this way not only with geographical communities, but also with specific cultural groups and interest groups.

Every cultural and interest group has its own energetic form and exists as a metaphysical entity. In some religious and spiritual circles, groups consciously tune into their fellows and colleagues all across the world, joining silently with them. In the silence, connected by vibration and energy, they build their inner community and build their solidarity.

In any spiritual celebration, it is possible to tune into all the other people in other places doing similar worship and celebration. Meditators can weave and connect the many different groups, and amplify their connection and vibration.

If you live in a small village or street or block of apartments, you can give calm time to contemplating the people, plants and animals who live in your community. By thinking of them, you begin to link them with energy and create the invisible web of community. This creates an atmosphere that can then ground in real relationships and community.

It is important to do this work from a meditative space which is balanced, detached and non-interfering. The attitude is one of pure and loving awareness. It is not one that in any way radiates energy from the meditator's physical body; no strain or dynamic energy is experienced.

Through doing this kind of inner work, through networking and amplifying the connection between people, you strengthen their calm and loving synergy. You help to bring in the incarnating energies of unconditional love and the resonance of the Avatar of Synthesis. Simply by sitting in silence and networking, by doing that in harmonic peace, you will create your own local communal and harmonic convergence. We would entreat you to work in this way.

Done regularly, in a rhythm that goes on many years into the future, you may bring about miraculous changes within your communities.

O

It is good to work this way too with the psyche of humanity as a whole. Spend regular time envisaging the global family.

With this work, it is interesting, inspiring and useful to give your awareness to the people and organisations who do good. You may bring into your contemplation and energy work the international statesmen and women, the global activists, who are doing good. You can also contemplate the benevolent organisations such as the Red Cross, United Nations and so on. You can also visualise those millions of people who travel – the tourists, business people, airline pilots and so on. You can also let guide your consciousness in the threads of connection through the internet. All of this links you with the flows and interconnections of humanity.

More than that, you can also contemplate the psyches of individual nations, the 'folk souls'.

We would like you to play with, in your imagination, all the various groups that you can imagine. See these groups connecting and radiating good vibrations.

If you yourself are a politician or a decision-maker involved in political work with groups, pause daily and become aware of all the things which we have just discussed. Be aware of your energetic connection with your colleagues and partners, and also with your political opponents. You are all part of the one community.

○

It would have a profound effect upon political relationships if political actors realised that along with their colleagues and opponents they are co-creators. As co-creators, their political antagonists are to be honoured as players within the same field. Conscious energy workers can help create the networking and synergetic aura between politicians by visualising them as players in one enjoyable and creative game benefiting humanity and Earth.

When communities become calm and silent, they create an ambience which allows in the energies of unconditional love and group synergy. These energies sink into the network of the community. They allow the community to become more telepathically connected. We ask meditators, individually or in groups, to hold this awareness for the political world, visualising 'enemies' as friends, visualising the creativity of political conflict.

This attitude to political conflict can also be applied to couples. Arguments and conflict can be understood as a constructive form of relationship. The crucial point is whether the conflict stings or harmonises. If meditative focus is given to creating the understanding that conflict leads to creative change and harmony, then that meditative thought can be grounded in the couple's real-life experience.

This same approach can be applied to group meetings and decision-making, in families and in organisations. How often are you frustrated by group decision-making and personal conflict? First, let the conflict feel playful in you. Let it begin solely in you and let it begin in the spirit of silence. Then see how your change in sensation transforms the synergy of the group.

With the incarnation of we Orbs and the Avatar of Synthesis, and the approaching closeness of the unconditional love energies, it is time for you also to feel more relaxed about the conflict that emerges naturally in couples and groups. The appropriate attitude towards conflict is understanding, not complaint or judgment. Do not have an attitude that attempts to make conflict disappear — in order to make you feel better. Fill conflict with Love.

5
Your Group Connections

To how many groups do you belong? You belong to so many.

In human science you recognise that there is a magnetic attraction and connection between objects which have a similar vibration and resonance.

You can become aware of the many different vibrations you carry and radiate. How many different aspects are there to your character? Each of these aspects has its own vibration.

Because of this vibration you are connected — energetically and telepathically — to all the other people who share that aspect of your character and its vibration. At its simplest, if you have a grumpy aspect you are connected to everyone else with a grumpy aspect! You form a group with them because, whether you like it or not, you share a similar resonance.

Human beings, therefore, are not simply members of groups to which they obviously belong. You all belong, energetically, to many, many groups. Each of these groups radiates an atmosphere into the general aura of humanity and Earth.

As an exercise you might choose, with pen and paper, to list the number of aspects that belong to your personality.

They all join up with the millions of others who share that personality trait and radiate a quality into humanity and Earth. This radiation may be harmful or benevolent.

If you have a competitive nature, you can imagine that you form a resonant group with all the others who have a competitive nature. This feeds into humanity. Within your workplace, be aware that if you have a competitive personality, you form a distinct group with all the others who are also competitive. You and your fellow competitors form a specific group. In the same way the office complainers too form an invisible energetic group. You belong to more than one group at the same time.

Equally, you may be a non-assertive and timid person, and therefore will form a group with all those types as well.

Is what you emanate constructive? Are you aware of it? Do you have friends with whom you can honestly discuss all this? Can you and your friends take responsibility for what you radiate?

Also, there are groups according to your work and interests.

If you are a clerk, you form a part of a planetary group of clerks. If you are a salesperson, you form a part of a planetary group of salespeople.

You can see, therefore, that at different levels and in different aspects, you form interlinking, interrelating, complex patterns of relationship — locally and globally — with all the various aspects of what you are. *This is true for everyone.* No one is excluded. The aggressive business executive in his Wall Street suite is in direct relationship with the aggressive seven-year old Chinese girl demanding a new silk dress for her doll. There are no separations.

People are connected with people. Frequently, if individuals were to understand clearly who it is that they are in group relationship with, they would be extremely embarrassed.

The ramifications of all this are quite interesting for those who are prepared to ponder on this in their meditations and contemplations.

In each distinct field of connection, in each distinct group, it is possible to take responsibility and to know that, second by second, you play your full part in the kaleidoscope of manifestation which is human life upon this planet.

Through these various energy connections, all individuals, via their groups, are interlinked. There are no individuals or groups that exist in isolation. This is not to deny either the uniqueness of specific group or individuals. It is only to point out that energy swims, dances and resonantly vibrates between all living beings upon the planet.

At the top of the business pyramid sits the chief executive, apparently alone in her/his decision-making power. This is the boss. Look just for a minute into the more subtle dimensions and you will see the various connections between that individual and other individuals within the web. There are connections with others all across the planet. How are they linked? Catch the various energy threads. There may be a thread of insecurity which binds that individual to millions of others.

This way of perceiving things brings all people into an awareness that you are living beings who are part of the one single unit, which is life upon this planet.

We would ask you then to be careful about yourselves and to ignore no part of your character.

6
Healing

We would like to discuss the healing in which we are involved and to clarify the nature of the new forms of healing — particularly psychological — which are now available.

From our perspective much disease is the result of psychological turmoil, of unconscious conflict between the inner purpose of the incarnating soul and the resistance of the daily personality. The resulting disharmony manifests in a form of an energy congestion, which then shows up psychologically or physically as illness.

These disharmonies often have their roots in ancient history and group karma.

All human beings carry these internal frictions. They are normal. Most illness therefore is normal and part of a process of growth and alignment.

It is, therefore, to be expected that human beings endure and experience illness and disease. The problem is not so much with the illness itself, but with the attitude of the individual to the disease. It is helpful to see the creative aspects of illness. Its creativity lies precisely in the fact that illness is so often an overt manifestation of the clash between the purpose of the inner self and the personality. Illness makes the clash explicit. It can no longer be ignored.

People often live their lives ignoring their soul's purpose. Good and useful illness wakes them up so that they cannot avoid the issue.

Illness then presents an overt and timely reminder of inner dissonance. It presents the sick person with an opportunity for change.

We are talking here about changing patterns of behaviour. Do you sincerely want to change? We are talking here about changing long historical threads of attitude, vibration and rhythmic expression in your incarnations. Often this is not easy.

O

Modern psychology has done much to reveal the hidden layers of reality which affect behaviour. It is limiting to understand these subconscious and unconscious layers as being restricted to this one life. They layers of psychological experience that make you who you are belong to many lives and many ancestors.

What has all this to do with Orbs?

We bring into the psychic field of humanity the opportunity for very rapid transformations of past patterns into the resonance of unconditional love, faster than has been known on this planet before. We are also talking about new modes of healing which can, in a few short hours, affect transitions which might previously have taken lifetimes. How can this be so?

There are extraordinary opportunities for healing available. These opportunities will be available for the rest of humanity's history upon Earth.

We encourage people to celebrate this and we claim that in this area of healing and therapy you have positive proof, perhaps more than anywhere else, that there are profound changes taking place within the psyche of humanity and Earth in general.

All across the Earth, people are experiencing subtle changes within the atmosphere and aura of the planet, experiencing the new resonances of the Cosmic Christ/ Buddha energies.

In the new healing and therapeutic techniques, this is all tangible. They can be so fast and effective.

People will by now be generally familiar with the basic nature of these therapeutic techniques. They allow the individual to re-experience ancient events, which may unconsciously dominate behaviour and attitude in the present.

These ancient events can belong to the childhood of this particular lifetime. But the most profound source events, which are the key to current patterns of behaviour, may go back many thousands of years.

As people in therapy re-experience these events, they cleanse them of their influence. This re-experience and cleansing of personal history is the major technique of the new therapies.

There is a second set of techniques, which works with ancient patterns that are locked into the energy and physical memory of the body. These techniques, working with healing vitality, release from the fabric of the physical and energy body the memory patterns of traumatic events. The methodology of many breath strategies works primarily with the use of high-powered energetic flows.

We would claim that we Orbs are, in a sense, responsible for the efficacy of these techniques. We are not claiming responsibility for inventing the actual techniques. But we are the electric networking dynamism without which these techniques would not be so effective.

Just as the great being who is the Avatar of Synthesis works at a macrocosmic level threading together the consciousnesses of all beings on Earth, so we work similarly at a different level.

In healing we network all the different aspects within a single individual.

It is our networking synergy in healing situations that enables the healing release which brings about fast and effective transformation. This is also a reflection of the stage which humanity has reached. This ability for fast release and change is a reflection of the good karma that humanity has built up for itself. This is indeed a time of change.

O

We wish to make clear the inner dynamics of the new healing. It is a grand claim that people can, in modern healing and therapy, work through historical patterns which in the past might have taken several years or even lifetimes. This is indeed the case.

As we Sparks incarnate into the individual's energy we create a new dynamic of multi-dimensional possibilities. We create a new connectedness within the individual. We join up and merge the body, emotions, mind and soul in one newly dynamised web.

It is our nature to be aware of each other continuously and simultaneously. Our empathetic and telepathic rapport ignores space and distance.

O

The moment that our vibration touches the psyche of a human being we create within that person the potential for multi-dimensional connection with all other life.

Prior to our incarnation, human beings existed, in consciousness, like icebergs. In order to touch those levels of consciousness deep below, awareness had to pass down through strange frozen areas. Awareness had to move down into another dimension from the air at the peak of the iceberg, down to the waters of the depth.

Our incarnation now creates an electric wave of subconscious awareness which expresses itself through the whole existence of your iceberg. We create within human consciousness the ability to experience everything you are more easily.

At the same time, because of our expansive ability to link into the auras of all humanity, we can create the network that links you with all the other beings who are connected with your history.

Now in healing and therapy, when you pass through the catharsis of reliving ancient events, you connect with the individuals and situations involved in the original event. We create empathic, not karmic, links with those involved in the original situation that caused your distressed pattern.

This eases your healing and also can heal those other people too.

O

There is another dynamic at work here. We help also to recreate your internal web. We link all the cells, molecules and memories at your different levels — physical, emotional, mental. No part of you is separate from any other part. This was always the case, that you are a holistic system, but with our help the integration is more immediate and flowing. In healing situations, therefore, a release in one part of you happens easily in other parts of you.

Adult human beings have little conscious awareness of the memories that are lodged within the physical and emotional body. Young children, on the other hand, have a greater fluidity. The movement between body, emotions and thoughts is much more fluid in children. There is easier communication and integration of the whole system.

We help to bring that easier flow to adults too.

Many people who might be identified as mentally disturbed are frequently like young children, experiencing a continuum between their feelings, emotions and thoughts. The mechanisms of repression and internal compartmentalisation are less rigid. Modern society, however, gives them few secure frameworks for expressing and playing with this fluidity.

The nature of the incarnation of the Orbs into the psyches of humanity is such as to support the playful continuum between all aspects of yourself, which is a natural part of your creaturehood and childhood.

O

It is often considered that the human personality is simply a construct of psychological attitudes. This is not the case. Your personality is not simply mental and attitudinal, it is also empathetic, sympathetic and instinctive.

Each personality has its own distinct sets of sentiments. Individuals have different ways of relating to and responding to landscapes or sunsets. Some people prefer cats and others prefer dogs.

Similarly, people have their own physical resonances in the way they relate to their planet, how you move through air, walk upon earth, or swim through water.

The experience now available to people is an awareness of yourselves as *total* creatures.

o

No matter your age or physical state, take time to become fully aware of the miracle which is your body. This miraculous machine moves you through time and space. As you walk down the street, be aware of the motion of your legs and the street passing beneath your feet as you push yourselves forward on the balls of your feet.

Become aware of the air brushing your face, of the temperature of the atmosphere against your skin. Notice that your eyes are seeing, your ears are hearing, your nose is smelling, that you are even tasting the air around you.

Be aware of your body. Be aware that your body is made up of many millions of cells and molecules, each one with a consciousness of its own, yet held together in the framework which is your consciousness. Be aware of this miracle.

Be aware of the spiritual nature of your cells and molecules as they too expand and move into divine light.

Become aware of the glory which is your emotional life, of the extraordinary depth of sentiment of which you are capable. Be aware of the deeply inspiring affection which you are capable of expressing — the sense of bonding within a family or loved ones, the way pets are cuddled, the way you may embrace a tree.

Be aware of the way in which music inspires you emotionally and sends currents through you. Be aware of how your whole body responds in a certain sentimental and empathic thrill to the resonance of the music. Be aware of your creativity that exists in your sentimentality and your emotions. Be aware of their purity and inspiration.

We do not feel that we need to encourage you to be aware of the glories of the human mind. That is too obvious, as the mind is the predominating note of your culture and out of balance.

Be aware of the way in which you are an integrated being. You are incarnate through your emotions, mind and physicality. You are not compartmentalised. You are everything that you are.

O

Your modern psychological theories are similar to your subatomic science theories. Beneath the surface hidden forces are at work.

These hidden forces, despite their invisibility, hold all the real power and influence.

Both the psyche and the atom are capable of high-powered energetic discharge. Nuclear explosion and nuclear power are paralleled by explosions of consciousness in human beings. Hidden forces are dynamic. Your psyche is capable of nuclear power.

This understanding of invisible dynamics makes it easier to understand how we Orbs work and function energetically.

Therapists and healers, in working with human beings, are dealing with energy beings. There are oceans of energy beneath the surface patterns and behaviours.

To enable healing and change, there must be a release of energy, like a quantum leap within the psyche of the individual. Quantum leaps are natural movements in energy between one state of consciousness and another.

Healers and therapists work as manipulators of energy and memory, and bring into consciousness ancient wounding events. These can then be transformed and discharged.

These healing techniques, however, have been constrained by the limitations of the time and space dimensions. Historically, individuals could heal only those experiences that belonged solely to them.

The incarnation of Orbs and the general repatterning of humanity's psychic culture by the Avatar of Synthesis allow healing to transcend the old time-space limitations.

As we wrote above, the potential for healing is enhanced at two levels. First, we create a new empathic web between all the aspects within you — emotional, mental, physical and spiritual, cellular and molecular.

This means that a release at one level within you or in one set of cells immediately affects all other levels and cells within you.

The second expansion comes because we have helped to network you more intimately with all the individuals and histories related to your history. As you heal a particular pattern, there is also a healing in the other beings who are in one way or another interwoven with that particular pattern.

There may, for example, be a past life pattern involving a small group of individuals who over a long period of time have chosen to incarnate as relations, parents, offspring, siblings, intimates, grandparents and so on. Over millennia, certain patterns of their individual karma are interwoven into a group karma. Now, in our present time, if one individual from that group goes into therapy — for example, a young woman whose pattern is a grievance against a particular parent — that young woman, as she releases herself through transformation and discharge of those original energies, releases not only herself but also creates a helpful wave of karmic release for the other people within that particular network of group karma.

If you as an individual clear yourself of a particular pattern, you are now also to a degree — though not completely — triggering and helping with the work of clearing that pattern within the whole group.

What we are talking about here is the specific disentangling of severe psychological difficulties that exist in the most intense and convoluted way in human groups.

By clearing your pattern and therefore helping to clear the patterns of others, you are in a dynamic energetic way forgiving them with a force of psychic power that also releases them.

This all has clear ramifications for healers and therapists, and for friends counselling and supporting each other. Be more sensitive to the network of relationships that you all have. Be aware of how important are all the other actors in the family and the story. Everyone is part of the cause, the story and the healing. You too, as friend and healer, are also obviously part of the story.

7

Psychedelic Healing Drugs

The purpose of this particular session is to discuss the nature of spiritual drugs in relation to human consciousness.

First, any drug is made up of molecules which, in their own way, carry consciousness — as do trees or rivers or plants. Different drugs work on different levels of the human body. The drugs which interest us here are those that affect the brain and its perceptions, those medicines that alter states of consciousness.

These medicines facilitate the brain in opening to the greater consciousness which exists 'out there'. They do this by working partly through how the brain accesses consciousness and partly through the way that the brain can influence sensations in the physical body.

They also work directly upon the electro-chemistry of the brain and the production of brain hormones. All this affects the frequency and harmonics of the brain.

A major function of brain cells, especially those upon the surface of the brain, is to act as receiving points or anchors for information that is more subtle and energetic than the five senses of touch, taste, sound, smell and vision.

This more subtle information radiates through space like sound or light waves, but is registered by the surface areas of the nervous system and brain. The conscious mind working through the brain, then has to register and interpret that information. Psychotropic medicines affect the brain so that it can more easily anchor down information that is usually inaccessible. The information is there to be received, but the brain and nervous system are not sensitive enough to perceive and register it. Psychotropic medicines change that.

○

When these medicines are taken with the intent of healing and spiritual development, then they are powerful allies in those efforts. Moreover, if we Orbs and the energy field of the Avatar of Synthesis are involved in the event, then there are the possibilities for intensely fast transformation, healing and expansions of consciousness.

In the same way, as we discussed above, that we can enable much deeper forms of spiritual experience and healing, so we too can deepen the effect of these medicines which open consciousness. Always noting that the intention is carefully guided so as to be healing and spiritually developmental.

○

In most cultures there have been groups of people who used plant medicine for these sacramental purposes. The experience placed the user in harmony with the essence of nature and the environment, and in glowing resonance with various forms of solar and cosmic energy. This was part of the natural priesthood.

The twentieth-century development and usage of

LSD and ecstasy is, at its best, just a reflection in a contemporary situation of these ancient medicines.

In a sense, just as the atomic bomb unlocked the full power of the atom, so LSD unlocked the power of the unconscious mind and its perceptions; often too dramatically. Both LSD and ecstasy were originally developed as therapeutic strategies but became part of mass healing ceremonies in which we Orbs were able to participate and enable collective experiences of blissful connection to the web of all life.

Both in flower power festivals and in raves, swarms of human souls connected through usage of these medicines in great tribal healings and celebration. Many people have awoken to the beauty of existence at these events. Be aware that these are mass events whose atmosphere and vibration were enabled by we Orbs and the field of the Avatar of Synthesis. We are sorry for those who were casualties of the experience too.

○

These medicines, if taken with care, can still be usefully used as gateways to development. They can be used both for personal healing and for the other healing that comes from being connected to the family of life in all dimensions. Flower power children recognised each other instantly. As do ravers. As do subsequent collectives of young people.

In the 1960s, many millions of young people experienced dynamic explosions of consciousness by taking psychedelic medicines. This dynamism was amplified by the new energies and beings flooding into Earth to enable group consciousness, synergy and planetary concord.

8

What You Can Do with Your Consciousness and Radiance

We want to offer practical applications.

The opportunities for group energy work and group development are intensified by our presence and the presence of the Avatar of Synthesis. We network and synergise your consciousness. We network and synergise your energy at all levels, cellular and of the soul.

This provides opportunities for living more gracefully upon this planet. We are supportive of your happiness and the acceleration of your human species' development.

Risking repetition, we facilitate a new reality for your relationship with yourself and with all other selves upon this planet. You are all linked and are one. This is now more deeply embedded in your actual experience and awareness. Divisiveness is reduced. For humanity this is a significant step. You have indeed always been linked at a soul level, but this sensation of unity was not a daily, ordinary experience.

We enable this growth and change in consciousness, but its full development requires your co-operation and effort. We want to explore what this co-operation and effort look like. We want you to experience us as friendly playmates. We are just a bit different because we have different histories.

So do not read what we are saying with any form of profound seriousness. Listen and hear carefully what is it that we wish to say, but listen and hear carefully as you would give your attention to a close friend. Believe us when we say that we have a profound affection and honour for you.

We are in awe of and celebrate the deep sense of compassion and sensitivity that you are capable of expressing as a species — and this is indeed a profound lesson for us.

What you can then value about us is our natural cosmic consciousness and our sense of the playfulness of all creation.

It might seem that we are closer than you to the source and mystery of all life. But you human beings have your own closeness to source — through your sentiment of compassion. It is Divine Compassion which not only holds all creation in being, but also draws all creation into the fulfilment of its potential.

We learn from you and you from us.

Please take seriously what we communicate and allow it to stimulate your awareness and expand your consciousness so you become more fully in tune with the true nature of the Cosmos.

We ask you to meditate upon the reality of this connection and the web and your own place within your groups. Do all this only if your intuition tells you that it has some value.

We have already suggested certain exercises for couples. We emphasise the care that two people need to give each other, with awareness of the vibrations they radiate at each other and the vibrations they radiate together to the outside world. This is ecological responsibility.

In the same way, we ask you as you to hold a similar awareness as you pass through your daily social and work life. Energy and synergy make life intimate. Be aware. Be responsible.

Our purpose is to underline the extraordinary relationship which you have with your environment and which your environment has with you.

As you move through your social life, be aware that the level of interaction which is apparent to your five senses is but the tip of an iceberg. Underneath all of it are vibrations and energy and intimate connection. This affects you and it affects other people. We ask you to be aware that the energy which you emanate as you walk into a crowd, the attitude which you put out, is felt in one form or another by the other individuals in that crowd. The energy that you radiate does not evaporate.

How often do you walk into a situation and monitor what quality you are radiating in that moment? Energy follows thought, feeling, emotion and attitude. Again, with care, take responsibility for your rhythm and oscillations.

Imagine a pleasant party. An individual enters that space and aggressively shakes hands with one person. The handshake is complete and finished, but the energy of the handshake reverberates through the room as a reality in its own right. The quality of energy in the handshake continues to exist until it is absorbed or transformed.

Now sense an embrace, a cuddle, a hug — and their quality of vibration. This too continues to exist. Different qualities of energy float around in clouds of a similar quality. People are influenced by these clouds.

O

The point we are trying to make must be clear by now. Can we ask you to put this awareness into your attitudes and actions?

We cannot demand this. We are attempting to

seductively call forth from you a natural and enjoyable sense of responsibility for the true being that you are, and for the effect that you have upon your environment. This will also add a beneficial dimension to your general experience of all realities.

The energy you radiate can affect all beings, so your major responsibility is to manage the vibrations of your mood. There may, or may not be, clear results. The results may occur years or decades or even centuries later. Be beautiful now.

Accept the lack of influence you have sometimes. You may be in a situation you do not like and cannot change. That can be absolutely fine. Your purpose is to be aware of what you radiate. That is your primary and major duty. It serves you and serves others.

○

We want to move on to the nature of astrological influences upon humanity and other cosmic energies that affect the planet.

Throughout history, mystics and astrologers have been fully aware that there are planetary and stellar energies which come into the planet and affect behaviour patterns, attitudes and atmosphere.

These astrological energies have a general effect. They influence groups, not just individuals. Many people can be affected similarly. For example, people who share a birth date might be influenced in a similar direction. Equally, a nation may have its own astrological character, so all its citizens may be influenced by particular stellar impulses.

This is another way of illustrating how everything in existence is interconnected and how groups of people are influenced to behave similarly.

The importance of this information lies in the fact that it can help you lose your sense of isolation and containment.

Often, your moods and feelings are not just your moods and feelings. They belong to a whole group of people who are having a similar experience. Knowing this can healthily melt your self-centredness and also provide comfort through the understanding that you are not alone in your experience. It expands your ego boundaries to include others. You become more like us.

For example, a particular stellar energy might radiate through to Earth and humanity, which creates the experience of tension, stress and depression in you. This is not enjoyable. But if you know that many other people are having a similar time, it becomes easier to manage. The depressed or anxious mood becomes less personal and more collective. Simply knowing that you are part of a collective experience and not isolated is relieving.

○

It is also good to be aware that astrological influences affect groups as much as individuals. Therefore, when you experience a particularly intense mood or mood swing, it may be helpful for you to pause and consider whether it is your experience alone or whether you are part of a collective astrological event.

Pausing to consider this takes you into an awareness that is good for you and for others. Pausing to consider this possibility can enable you to centre and calm yourself more easily. Through empathy and connection, your calming helps all the others experiencing that same influence also to find their centre and calm. Your pausing heals both yourself and the collective. You expand your consciousness to include and empathise with others. You develop compassion and love.

So let us emphasise this message: when you experience an unusually strong mood, stronger than usual, pause and take time to contemplate whether it is just yours or if it belongs to everyone.

See how this helpfully melts self-centredness.

With the incarnation of us Sparks and the incarnation of the Avatar of Synthesis the connections are amplified. The astrological influences can be more powerful.

Suppose an energy comes through — perhaps associated with Pluto or Saturn — that influences you all so that you feel the tensions of your past and the restrictions of time and space. This is very uncomfortable even though it is an opportunity for development.

Imagine that at the same time another energy comes through which vibrates with the new Aquarian frequency of fluidity and surfing the waves of consciousness and connection. This new Aquarian frequency can also create tension as people have to release Piscean patterns of safe devotion.

So here we have two energies coming into Earth and humanity, both of them creating tension for you. The first takes you into a sensation of compression. The second takes you into the tension of releasing old safety for new fluidity.

This kind of astrological event happens regularly. It creates a disturbing and intense tension for you. But, as we said above, everybody is experiencing a similar effect.

The moment that one of you passes through the point of tension into a new, more developed state, your transformation is felt by the collective. Especially those people who have a similar psychological make-up to you will experience relief and be able more easily to make the personal development themselves. When someone else develops, it helps you. When you develop, it helps others. This is the foundation of group process, group change and group initiation.

You therefore have a responsibility to respond in a wise and intelligent way when you experience great discomfort, knowing that your response affects others.

This requires conscious awareness.

Here follows something which we know will encourage and interest you. The human beings who are now liberated from the cycle of rebirth and are fulfilled in love, compassion and consciousness — they too can feel the new energies that come into Earth and humanity. They too work with these new frequencies, seeking to help the rest of you who have not been liberated. If you want, you can choose to be in harmonic resonance with these liberated human beings and allow yourselves to feel their way of working with the new frequencies. Just open your consciousness to the possibility of being connected with these loving elders, these older members of your human family.

When next you are in disturbing tension, pause and open yourself to the Buddha or Christ or Kuan Yin or any other being you feel is elevated, and how they are responding to the astrological influences. Allow this contemplation to be felt and cellular. This can be beautiful and healing.

○

You are not alone.

We ask you to be aware too of your responsibility to those who are less aware than you.

We ask you also to accept that there are other consciousnesses far more aware than you.

With all of these companions, you work together creating a new network and a new world.

O R B S S P E A K

9

Between Groups and Groups

As individuals you have connections with each other. You also have your connections with various groups.

Groups also have connections and relationships with other groups.

Seen from an inner perspective, groups behave like individuals, like big human beings. Groups have distinct personalities and attitudes. This is, for example, very clear if you look at national characters.

As souls you choose to incarnate into these national characters as part of your learning and development.

As stellar energies come into the planet whole nations react. The whole country is filled with people having a similar set of emotions and attitudes. But different countries have different temperaments. The influence on the English may be different from the influence on Brazilians.

As profound waves of new energy pass through Earth whole nations are influenced in different ways, some thrown into turmoil, others into productivity, some into passivity, others into aggression.

In a human body, a change in one of your cells can affect all the cells in the system. This is important, for example, in healthcare.

In a group of people such as a family or team, a change in just one of the individuals has an effect throughout the group. This influence is not only like a domino or ripple effect. It also comes from within. A change inside one of you is also a change inside the rest of you. You are all always in another dimension of which you are unaware. Within this dimension, you are all within each other.

Groups also affect other similar and connected groups. Clans affect clans. Teams influence other teams. Nations within the global family affect each other. But these influences are not just the usual ones that you recognise in external and visible relations. They happen within a psychic and energetic dimension that is very intimate and familiar. It is as intimate as brothers and sisters, couples and lovers.

When a nation behaves in a certain way, similar behaviour is felt and emerges from within other nations. Political groups have intimate rapport no matter how much their appearances may differ. This infuence is cellular and telepathic.

O

We suggested earlier that couples pause to contemplate what atmosphere they radiate as a couple into the environment. We suggested that they take conscious responsibility for their radiation.

This suggestion is also very relevant to groups.

It is possible for a group to take time out and reflect on the energies they put out to their local environment.

Imagine workers in a shop sitting down on a weekly basis to discuss the collective influence and the effect their atmosphere has on their local community. This is not a far-fetched idea. There are many holistic, health and spiritual centres and shops who could do this and do it already.

It also makes sense to imagine the staff of a school sitting down regularly to assess their collective resonance and its effect. This could include students. The groups within the school — teachers, students, administration, maintenance and so on — could also contemplate the effect they have on each other, what they emanate and how it influences the other groups.

This is a high level of self-awareness that could be brought into operation. We are painting the picture of a potential scenario, sophisticated and elegant in its aware-ness. It will come. The evolution of your consciousness, your natural connection with all life, and our support, make it inevitable.

○

Today it is possible for all groups and communities who are in any way spiritual to adopt this way of looking at things and to accept your responsibilities. You can monitor the quality of your purpose and of your relationships — and not just the visible products.

Let us be clear that the dynamism of the energy which you reverberate out into the atmosphere is extremely powerful. It has a direct effect upon other groups. You are all in dynamic inter-relationship. You exist within each other, as do we.

The influences of a hostile group are obvious. A couple in hostile relationship pollute and negatively affect their wider family and friends. A nation whose internal politics are hostile also has a terrible influence.

And if you, as observer, have a negative judgment on these hostile couples or hostile nations, then you too —

through your judgment — are drawn into the hostility. You become part of their hostile influence and help build that hostility with your own criticism and negative vibrations.

It is helpful if you take responsibility for your part in creating public opinion. 'Public opinion' is the mood of a nation or a culture and can have benevolent or destructive effects.

In politics it is the style and mood of the political process which is usually more important than the policies themselves. It is in the mood that you find the energetic dynamics that play out into external relations and effects.

As the effect of the Avatar of Synthesis increases, so this dimension becomes more important.

You are a member of the national group into which you were born. For example, if you emanate a particularly intense patriotic energy, this will influence and affect all other people within your national group. If at a subjective level you have an attitude of detachment from nationalism, then that pattern reverberates out to the group.

See what your national group is radiating into the world community. It is important for individuals to recognise, particularly in the problem area of international politics, that they are a part of a national group. Your own, apparently private, subjective attitude towards your nationality has an effect on the total national attitude. Energy follows thought and, in your own private way, you can work within the great arena of international relations.

Although you may find these political realities sombre, remember too that there are innumerable groups and influences throughout Earth and Cosmos that are beautiful and radiating love. There are innumerable networks working in multi-dimensional fields, whose sole purpose is to emanate joy, love and creative peace to all other groups.

This is worth meditating on. It will feed your soul.

It is also good to spend time contemplating those exquisite groups of multi-dimensional beings whose beauty you can hardly understand and whose purpose is to be glorious flames of continuous energy stimulating, healing and regenerating all life on Earth.

O

We are painting a picture of the dynamic interdependence and intimate connection between all life-forms upon this planet.

This intimacy also exists between all life-forms throughout the Cosmos.

All consciousnesses, no matter how unique and sophisticated, are connected. In their own way they too form groups and networks. Imagine that every sun/star has a consciousness and that every constellation or galaxy is a group. As groups they radiate atmospheres which are very different from that which they radiate as single entities.

The whole is always greater than the sum of the parts — and the *quality* of the whole is always different from that of the sum of the parts.

With human beings, with your species, this amplified radiation that comes from groups can obviously be for good or for bad. Some groups emanate a destructive and polluting atmosphere far worse than any produced by individuals. The pack mentality can be corrosive. Other groups radiate care and beauty, transcending the limitations of the individuals.

Our work is to attract you to be aware of your group relationships and always, within the group, to radiate more beauty and love than you do as separate units. Can you resist such an opportunity?

The purpose of this book is to attract you the reader into an awareness of your invisible relationships and the effect of your consciousness. Perhaps you want to reject all these ideas, but — like it or not — you are energetically a living part of group consciousness. No matter how much you pride yourself on your own individuality, you are also dancing and entwined and expanded in group consciousness.

○

You have patterns of relationship which connect you with many different groups simultaneously. You have connections which are historical and you belong, from the perspective of reincarnation to groups of friends and family. You sometimes incarnate as a group and experience collective karmic patterns. Within these groups, when any single individual develops and transforms, this vibrates to release other people from the same pattern.

You are also connected to groups of souls who have a similar stellar, astrological and cosmic vibration. You are connected to those people who have similar souls to your own.

This may be a new awareness for many readers. Your soul vibrates in a particular way depending upon the circumstances and environment in which it first emerged from the Cosmic Breath.

Souls form connections with other souls of a similar resonance. This shows up in the way that people incarnate, develop and then draw back into the Ocean of Source. Each individual is a unique soul, but you also share certain characteristics and tones with other souls.

As souls, moreover, you exist in a way that is similar to we Orbs.

As souls you are completely attuned and resonant

with each other. You are, as souls, completely group-aware because your consciousness as souls is in an energy field of unity and harmony.

Our job is to help you in your daily lives become aware of what you experience *as souls*. In good moments of altered consciousness you experience this mystic unity with other souls. In this experience of mystic unity you fully understand the reality of group consciousness. In mystic unity you know everything is interconnected and of one source. You could choose to acknowledge this more often.

Sometimes these soul groups are called Rays. You are linked to all other souls on your Ray. Again the synergy of development and liberation is at work here. When one of you within a Ray group moves forward and liberates yourself from a certain pattern, that liberation echoes out through the whole of your soul group, through the whole of your invisible ashram. You are a member of a multi-dimensional ashram. This is your true home and soul group. You work together in a telepathic manner and you meet together when your body is asleep and you are in your dream bodies.

Again, our purpose here is to dynamically stress the interdependence and profound intimacy that exist between you and your fellows in your ashram. When any of you move slowly along the spiritual path it slows all of you. When you move with grace and speed, you all shift. We Sparks support you in this.

Within your Ray group, within your Ashram, be encouraged because there are some consciousnesses far evolved from where you now sit. Their radiation and on-going expansions serve you.

10

Animals, Plants, Minerals, Cosmic Beings and Human Beings

We want now to bring to your attention the patterns of relationship within the group consciousness of the planet as a whole — the relationships that exist between the different realms in nature. We specifically want to discuss the natural realms of the mineral, plant, animal, human, the super-human and the devic-angelic realms.

We want, as always, to take a set of intellectual ideas and to make them more experiential for you. We also want to motivate you with the reality that you are living second by second within what we might call a 'spiritual ecology'. In a sense it would be possible to retitle this book, 'Spiritual Ecology'.

We have discussed in some detail the relationship and the energetic aura that is put out by two individuals in a coupling relationship, and that which exists within small and large groups.

We are concerned here with the relationships that exist between the realms in nature.

There are several levels from which these relationships can be surveyed — from the scale of the total planet through to that of the individual.

Let us begin by observing the total planet.

From an external perspective we might see that the major life-form that dominates the planet is its dense physical body, the mineral realm of the planet as a whole. Earth is a solid material planet. There are other planets where there is hardly any dense materialised form. In fact there are planets and systems which are pure energy and which cannot be seen by a human eye.

The body of Earth is made up of minerals and of the consciousnesses of mineral elemental life. You refer to these elemental lives in various ways such as gnomes and dragons. These beings are your human representation of the undulating consciousness of the dense mineral planet.

The consciousness of this dense mineral body of the planet responds to lengthy cycles of time and pressure. In a sense, gravity and time are the major forces which work to effect the changes of consciousness in the collective consciousness of the mineral kingdom.

But this collective mineral consciousness is also made up of many lesser beings, which manifest through all the various forms of the mineral realm: metals, rocks, crystals and so on. These different types of mineral represent a chain of development until some of the radioactive metals seem to transcend form, time and space.

We are drawing your attention to the aliveness and consciousness of the mineral kingdom. This is part of your community on Earth. They belong in your group — and you to theirs.

This is more obvious with the plant and animal kingdoms. But we draw to your attention to both the collective consciousness of species and types, and the consciousness of the individual plants and animals.

From one perspective, outside of time and space, you are all one vast being — planet, minerals, plants, animals, humans. You flow together through time and space. Your physical bodies are made up of each other. You are one organism containing many smaller individual ones. You may seem separate but you are not. Your whole system, like us, is one great group moving together, changing together.

We are all the manifestation of a single breath of creation, a breath that is vibrant, active, interconnecting and embracing in one great and single awareness.

○

Circulating through the plant kingdom, from the tiniest seed to the most glorious redwood tree, are currents of wind, of air. These currents, these elemental consciousnesses, flow around, above and beneath the plants, the animals, and humans. Air is gaseous mineral life. You are surrounded by it. It pulses into you, this external life, these external elemental air beings, to be absorbed and become you.

Notice also the flow of water all around you — water is flowing mineral life. Look how much water there is in your body. You can understand here the experiential intimacy of nature's realms. In physical form, there is no separation, only a dance, a continuum. In a very clear biological sense, the human is indeed animal. In a clear chemical sense, the human is indeed mineral. Look also at the food chains. These are all intimate relationships.

The physical environment determines, in an ecological sense, the plant and animal life which can exist within it. The plants and animals then engage in their own sets of relationships, which are of mutual benefit. In these cycles the general rhythms of growth, explosion, decay and decline are helpful and necessary.

The human realm, however, provides, as a whole — and we are thinking here of the many millions of beings incarnated upon the planet — a dynamically new and different form of swirling psychic life which moves, dancing, tornado-ing across the surface of the planet.

You human beings tornado yourselves through life, furrowing your way through the plant and animal realms. These furrows can be seen not only in small rows where seeds can be sown, but also in huge channels which are the conduits for cars, trains, ships and planes.

The human realm also penetrates the Earth realm in its removal of minerals from Earth and in the banging, melting and electrifying of them into new shapes and forms of mineral life.

In its most extreme form we can see the relationship between humanity and mineral life exemplified in the conversion of mineral life into energy. This energy then flows into great factories and industries which are only of benefit to the human species.

This activity is paralleled by the dynamic psychic energy you create. You all make noise. It is getting louder. We want you to perceive the power of the mass psyche of humanity and the way in which it smothers and engulfs the planet.

The psychic atmosphere created by human beings penetrates the winds and the dancing air of the planet, and penetrates the movement of the waters through the planet. Your psychic vibrations affect the weather.

Humanity directly affects the air and the water and the mineral kingdoms. Be aware of your individual psychic effect and the psychic effect of the whole of humanity as you touch and move the mineral realm in cars, domestic appliances and the concrete and metal which make up modern buildings. Also, how you touch the plant realm for food and fuel and clothing. And animals too.

Why not pause and assess the quality of humanity's relationship and vibrations towards the mineral, plant and animal realms. Your psychic attitude affects the mineral kingdom, manifesting through deep vibrations that undulate through the whole consciousness of the kingdoms which are Earth's body.

This impact on the mineral kingdom can result, in extreme situations, in mass mineral reactions in the form of tidal waves, earthquakes and volcanic activities. And in benevolent effects too.

O

You live in an extremely subtle and sensitive interrelationship with the realms around you. Your personal psychic atmosphere influences the health of your pets and your plants. It also influences and creates the general atmosphere in your home and your workplace. Your psychic ambience also affects the general atmosphere of your block of apartments or your street or village and goes outwards, affecting the atmosphere of the whole planet.

Be aware of what you create. This is one of the most fundamental lessons of spiritual ecology — that you have to take responsibility for your effect on the beauty and harmony of your surroundings. This requires a tangible, daily effort to be caring towards these realms. Your vibrations anchor into the mineral, animal and plant life which surrounds you. Monitor your moods. Are you responsible for psychic pollution? It is sensible to be careful. With the new group synergy and connections this is increasingly important for the progress of all life.

Radiate kindness into your psyche. Be aware that you are a unit within the mass psyche of humanity and, as such, working towards melting, or building, the mass karma and experience of humanity.

Be aware of the throbbing cellular life that moves through leaves and flowers — and the aroma and magnetism of these plants. The plants affect you. You affect them.

Remember the consciousness that incarnates in animals.

Know equally the dynamic life that exists in the very molecules and atoms of the homes in which you live. Be aware of the consciousness and the life within the ground and minerals upon which you walk and which is also your home.

We are not asking you to develop a romantic trance so as to drift through life. We are suggesting that, in an ordinary daily way, you be aware of your environment.

Be aware of the general trends and atmospheres that exist, with you, in your locality and on the whole planet. Remember the interpenetration, the interrelationship, between the realms. And, if you wish, you may in your meditation choose to radiate out into these various relationships harmony, love, affection and friendship and a general sense of happy spiritual co-operation.

O

This all happens too at a stellar and cosmic level. Astrology is the science of the relationships between cosmic energies.

Earth is a huge, dynamic, radiating energy being. There is more than just the physical body of the earth. There is more than the electromagnetic, electric and pranic body. Earth's body includes all the energies and consciousnesses of the mineral, plant, animal and human beings. Some of this is visible, but there are also all the invisible realms and beings and dynamics.

The souls who are incarnate upon Earth create a huge energy realm of their own at many levels of energy and consciousness — all dynamic and radiant. Earth is a throbbing being of extraordinary energy.

And Earth is but one part in a total system.

At its centre is the Sun which has its own wonderful sets of energies and, orbiting around the Sun, the planets which, together with it, form this total Solar System.

The Solar System is, at its level of energy, fantastically more dynamic and radiant and throbbing than Earth and her realms. Your solar system is a cosmic entity radiating intense, dynamic forms of electric consciousness. This consciousness connects with all the other star systems.

You are part of this. Of course you are connected with star beings and extra-terrestrials. That is part of being an inhabitant of this Cosmos.

Just as you have a soul, so your solar system has a soul too. So too does the galaxy and other star systems.

The souls of stars are in intimate communication with each other. They speak to each other.

When your ancient peoples gave the planets and constellations names and saw them as human-like gods, this was not mythic but factual. These are indeed real beings. These beings communicate.

We have described the way in which your groups need to be aware of the energy which they radiate. We suggested that you be reflective about this. At their own level of consciousness, the vast consciousnesses and personalities that make up planets, star systems and cosmic systems are also aware of the energy which they emanate as a system or a group, and which they feed into the total system of which they are part.

At their level of consciousness there is an intimate understanding of the atmosphere and energies being expressed throughout the Cosmos. This intimacy is electric and continuous, in time and space, and also transcending time and space. The consciousness of a stellar being is absolutely sensitive to that which it radiates. It perceives it as it happens.

Because of this network of cosmic and multi-dimensional connections, Earth is influenced by all these beings and their radiations. You, humanity and Earth's other kingdoms are all influenced and connected. And, in reverse, the Cosmos is influenced and touched by Earth, by humanity and by you.

O

Humanity, as it moves purposefully forward through time and space, reaches points of crisis and need. This is just like a human being. When in crisis, humanity creates a vacuum of need.

The consciousness of your solar system and the consciousness of your galaxy, and all that is part of it, is completely aware of humanity's need. Earth communes with Sun. Your Sun communes with other stars, other solar systems, other galactic systems.

All these great beings understand and experience, through continuous communication, through a non-stop intimate electric relationship, the needs within your solar system, the needs of humanity.

Somewhere in the Cosmos there is an energy or con-sciousness appropriate to meet humanity's requirements and ease the challenges. Sometimes called Avatars these beings enter your galaxy, your time-space dimension, your solar system, your Earth, and finally the energy field of humanity itself — and you.

Indeed, we began this communication by describing how we ourselves accompany the Avatar of Synthesis, who is just such a response from another star system to the needs of humanity.

At this moment in time-space, humanity cannot progress easily through its next stages of growth.

Humanity's next stage of growth is to achieve a new level of group consciousness and synergy. Synergetic consciousness of itself and all other beings in the community of life. Not simply as an intellectual idea, but as an experience. We the Sparks, the Orbs, along with the Avatar of Synthesis, are here to facilitate.

○

We are also very happy to communicate about your current ecological crisis. From our perspective we see no crisis that is different from the usual ones your species has experienced in the past.

We have already explained in this writing how human beings are more friendly with nature than with each other. We also want to remind you how you are all nervous creatures often trying to pretend to be solid. You are small creatures of the Earth and connected to the Cosmos. You are vulnerable animals with cosmic consciousness.

It is within a state of nervousness, within some understandable anxiety and fear that many of you are over-dramatic about what you perceive to be an environmental crisis.

There have been many Earth changes in the past. There

have been many changes in climate. They always bring affects to humanity and the other kingdoms on Earth. And Earth and her kingdoms survive and grow.

The real growth is always one of consciousness. Do you think Earth prepared herself so beautifully for all your incarnations only to reject you when there is a crisis? You sometimes have little idea of the beauty of Earth and her power. You have all emerged from her. The current population explosion is a plan carefully hatched by Earth. It is all to do with the growth in consciousness of the Earth and her realms as one great system which includes humanity.

The population explosion is no mistake or accident. And you, humanity, are fully aware of its effects and have done remarkably well in adjusting your food production in order to feed each other. You are also adjusting to the environmental effects of your population and industrial growth. You know what to do and are beginning to do it. So your situation, beneath the apparent crisis, is graceful.

The crisis that does exist is the crisis that has always existed. It is humanity's lack of co-operation and care for each other. The crisis is in the disparities of food and wealth, and the children and adults who do not eat or have no opportunities. This is the perpetual, enduring human crisis — to look after each other. We have described how we and the Avatar of Synthesis are here to help. Also, many other consciousnesses and beings support Earth and you.

The kinds of people who read a book like this are also the kinds of people who campaign for ecological sustainability. We support your campaign, but we would ask you to follow the guidelines of this book and recognise the crucial importance of the vibrations you radiate about this perceived crisis.

If you vibrate fear or urgency, then you are polluting

Earth's psychic atmosphere. This psychic pollution makes it more difficult both to achieve a practical solution to physical pollution and also to expand your consciousnesses. There is, as we say, a negative drama sometimes in the campaigning movement that may not be helpful.

The Cosmos loves Earth and humanity. Do not get lost in fears that mainly resonate with past wars and disasters. You live in a time of growing consciousness and opportunity. Many of you are creating good solutions to the problems that are only the natural outcome of change and transformation.

Be aware of the vibrations you radiate. Amplify your patience, your love and your optimism. And make the changes you need to make. Develop the answers. Look after each other.

○

On that note we wish to conclude this communication.

We hope that we have been clear and helpful. Our purpose is to support you in becoming more aware of yourself, your consciousness and your energy — on your own and in your groups.

Printed in the United Kingdom
by Lightning Source UK Ltd.
130693UK00001B/100-546/P